LAKE ERIE BLUE

Susan Grimm's poems practice what they preach. "Think interior like a geode," commands her concluding poem in *Lake Erie Blue*, and we recognize in that line the crystalline brilliance shining at the heart of each of Grimm's poems. Her subjects range from an explosive shipwreck in Lake Erie to quiet shipwrecks of desire; from the "inexplicable pink tinge of joy" to the slow, dark days of grief. And the language of *Lake Erie Blue* is as vast, startling, and unpredictable as the great body of water the book is named for. Grimm's adventurous music makes each poem, line by line, "all voyage, surprise."

    —Lynn Powell
        author of *Old & New Testaments* and *The Zones of Paradise*

In these accomplished, understated poems Susan Grimm wonderfully achieves two things that would seem mutually exclusive: the vivid and convincing evocation of her family life in its ordinary, working-class setting, and the simultaneous transformation of this material into an exciting aesthetic experience full of surprise and mystery. As Grimm lovingly pulls out past sights, sounds, smells, and feelings like treasures discovered in the attic—the small joys and griefs of growing up in a dingy Midwestern industrial town take on a larger meaning. Lake Erie is always on the horizon—seductive, treacherous, shallow, unfathomable. Grimm never tells too much, but she savors every word: one of the pleasures of this volume is the masterly play of her language.

    —Leonard Trawick
        Former director, Cleveland State University Poetry Center

LAKE ERIE BLUE

POEMS

SUSAN GRIMM

BkMk Press
University of Missouri-Kansas City

BkMk Press
University of Missouri-Kansas City
5101 Rockhill Road
Kansas City, Missouri 64110
(816) 235-2558 (voice)
(816) 235-2611 (fax)
bkmk@umkc.edu
www.umkc.edu/bkmk

Cover and book design: Nick Serafin
Author photo: J. Grimm
Production Staff: Ben Furnish (managing editor), Susan L.
Schurman (assistant managing editor), Michelle Boisseau (associate
editor), Bill Beeson, Dennis Conrow, Sandra K. Davies, Eugene
Murphy, Nick Serafin
Printing by Technical Communications Services, North Kansas City,
Missouri

Financial assistance for this project was provided by the Missouri Arts
Council, a state agency.

Library of Congress Cataloging-in-Publication Data
Grimm, Susan.
    Lake Erie blue : poems / Susan Grimm.
        p. cm.
ISBN 1-886157-46-4
        I. Catholics--Poetry.
        II. Family--Poetry.
        III. Erie, Lake, Region--Poetry.
        IV. Cleveland (Ohio)--Poetry.
        V. Europe, Central--Poetry.
PS3557.R4936 L+

                                2004003224

To the girl with long brown hair, Mary Grimm, sister and first reader.

ACKNOWLEDGMENTS

I wish to thank the editors of the following magazines where these poems first appeared.

Blue Mesa Review: "From the Sandy Bottom of Lake Erie: the G. P. Griffith"

Faultline: "Secrets of Murano"

Heliotrope: "Blue," "Recruits at Fort Stark"

The Montserrat Review: "The Peeling Away of Hands"

Pivot: "Harsh Summer Days"

Poetry Northwest: "Aunt Bella," "Green Wave," "Lake Erie Love Song," "Surely Incense and Mercy Will Follow Us All the Days of Our Lives," "Without Tongues: Family Stories"

Rattapallax: "Every Bad Thing That Could Happen"

West Branch: "Self-Portrait: Notes"

White Pelican Review: "Ninety-first Birthday Wish"

Willow Review: "The Dream of Soup"

"Ranunculacious" appeared in the anthology *The Poetic Image*.

CONTENTS

I

II

III

IV

I

GREEN WAVE

June 23, 1882. A wave rises out of the smooth, green
pan of Lake Erie—two miles long, eight feet high—
it rushes over Cleveland. No storm, no wind; barges
scrape on the pavement, fish gasp in the streets.
Eugenie, just then being born in Central Europe,

is squeezed out in a gush of fluid and blood.
How she became we all know—nine months before
pleasure rippled, fastened, and jumped. In the same
country, Stefan drinks. It's a warm morning,
but the metal cup is still cool in his hands.

In Scotland, Gemma's washing her hair. Her mother
holds the lip of the jug to her neck, and the water
fans out over the curling delta. William
lives shielded by the trees, already hidden
in the hills of West Virginia, his voice cut off

by the noises of the river he has yet to cross.
I've seen their pictures. Negatives darken
and curl in the basement. But even as the images
flattened and framed, the living shattered
the glass, swam out of the chemicals, alive.

It surprises me to give them sweat and shiver,
silence and scream. They have not visited
me in the night, ghostly hands rising
to beg for the poem of their dog, their house,
their china cup. Their knives and forks acted out

the story of their lives, dancing every day
on the table. They have not asked for that poem.
Like some magic, optical cloak, the past falls

from their shoulders as they labor along. It leaves
a tunnel behind, a canal, a ravine, a maze,

the ball of memory rolling through those years
like an unlit pinball. With Bill it hits a wall—
silence in the roar of the mill. Lou courts
memory, cuts windows, constructs her past
like an approved picture from the Advent calendars

of her youth. Also, Mitch Miller's bouncing ball—
coy indicator, chief sunbeam of the silvery moon's
stock schemes and passions—can be blamed for a lot.
Better that dot should be sun on water, sliding
the scallop from crest to trough. Last summer:

I sit on a beach; I wade a lake thinking
my secret dreams, thinking that I'm the point
of the arrow speeding into the future, when
I've already branched, become ridiculous
to the young. Even knowing, I want that steely point

dug in. To this Ohio beach with its secrets,
the waves come—each wave so brief, so chancy
in composition, transparent pale green
risen—the wind at their backs, the suck beneath.

White Horse in the Graveyard
—William and Gemma, grandparents

Isn't love supernatural? The moon over the road
shines round as the sundial in the garden
which lies about time—hot, late May scent

of early roses. Too much light still when
they move from parlor to porch. Her glasses
wink once with the moon; she takes them off.

Every shift of his body makes the wicker
creak. Intensified, he strides home, his face
flickering in the uneven light. The clouds,

serene, ornament the sky like her lace collar,
filmy waist—she dances above him, the sudden dark
fall of her hair. Her voice—but she is back there,

braided into the snow-white billows of her night
gown, the window open but she is firmly shut
now. The sound is louder than a sigh. Dizzied,

the living man passes the graveyard. Something
white moves behind the trees. Petals
neat and white as rice trickle down—bloom,

shift. It's a horse come over the stone
wall, beckoned under the stars by the smell
of fresh dirt and cut grass. But what

did the walker first believe? His heart throbs
at the ready, steadies as the milk-white horse
whickers, lowers its head to the grass, stands still

as the man approaches with his hand outstretched.

FAMILY ALBUM

Don't listen to her. Seventy years ago her daddy
visited and saw my sons, grown men in a cage.
What did he know with his milk smooth skin?
One visit to his cousins. I saw them every day.

We were good people; we worked hard. If there hadn't
been two boys, slow, at the same time—. Let me say
how we kept them in the kitchen, and not so
they didn't scare company. It was warm there and full

of light and smelled good from bread or bacon
or coffee. They were sweet and mindful, but not
remembering. Luke sang to Matthew, mostly hymns
without words but no less beautiful. Nothing

was wrong with their limbs. Long before
they grew taller than me and more melancholy,
we shut them up, their hands off the oven door,
their fingers out of the hinge. Every day

they'd had to learn again about the horse-startle,
the saw-bite. The way a child will jam his head
in the corner of his crib in sleep, they grew
used to their pen. I could have sent them away.

I could have let them wander and drown. You can
hear the river in the spring. They would have liked
the light-play, the icy shock, their clothes
darkening and floating, their laughter

rising hectic. There's a door on a house to keep
things private. Let her tell her own tale.

MAGIC BEANS

—Eugenie and Stefan, grandparents

I.

Old woman with thin white braids. She has shut
the back gate. She is not wise. She has one
golden earring, the hole for the other long closed.
For each rose planted in the yard, a child
goes into the world and brings back love.
Her legs are stretched out before her. This dying
takes so long. This dying does not matter.
She waits for the absence of breath to make her new.

II.

Letters she's received:
        Our Mother is dead—across the sea
like a star winking out—that far away—
but the night is darker, hence the black border.
        I'll send for you and the children—
no note on the table when he left, but two months
later a postcard of Squirrel Hill stuck
in an envelope, the flap not quite reaching.
        We've found work, Mother. Come
to Cleveland as soon as you can.

III.

She is walking the straight mown lane cut
from a tangle of saplings, sumac, pigweed,
morning glory vine. The whole weight of her
strikes firm on her two small feet. At the top,
if she turns, the woods will be at her back,
like the Carpathian forests where her father
disappeared each Monday bearing an axe. Now,
on her right—the easily observed space,
the hay bound up, the undulating backs of the hills.

IV.

How in the night he lay down, variable as dusk.
Later the good pain of the child tearing out,
her screams, the slick and bloody sheets.
Not necessarily acts of love, more like magic
beans—husband as peddler—making someone
who stays; pillar to the roof of family, wheel
to the wagon of home. Promise her birds
to peck out his eyes, elves that slice off
his tongue, gods who root him like a tree, hands
jerked up—fluttering—away from her skin.

PEACH FUZZ
—Lou's Sister

Of necessity Sylvie worries about the appearance
of things. So when trapped at the fence kneeling,
her hands full of weeds, her shoulder in its
perpetual shrug, she stays. Mrs. Berrey pushes

her story out. "I've been having trouble down there
for a long time, even before the girls." Behind her
the skinny Berrey kids yap over jacks. "This time
they just took it all out—the works!" Mrs. Berrey

leans forward, hisses: "I don't miss it a bit."
Sylvie's stomach blisters and shrivels. Maybe
it's kneeling too long makes her feel this way.
Sylvie thinks of last night, Herbert touching

her arm, the golden hairs. Peach fuzz, he'd said,
as if she were produce, a fruit, some miracle
of ripeness. What if it were him on his knees—
Sylvie stands—his hand on her arm, she swelling

like a gourd at the hospital where they scoop
you with metal spoons and tongs. At her sister
Meredith's wedding they made melon balls
all morning at the sink, seeds spilling out,

their arms slimy with juice; cutting perfect
orange globes from the canteloupe flesh.
Mrs. Berrey talks on into the night. Fireflies
punctuate her organs, her valedictory pain.

1932: DEPRESSION ERA CHOICES
—Lou

What is required? That she listen, that she
wipe, that she lean inconspicuous. She is not
thinking about the food smell in her hair,
the way the plates slide on the tray, the sad
eyes over their cheap potatoes. She fills
their cups with more coffee so she can
stay awake. What happens if she goes
downstairs—two alone, the store room dark?

Mr. B. imagines she smells like clover, not
that it matters. He will swallow her
whiteness, leave invisible marks on what
is curved and ironed and starched. The girls
nudge each other as he mouths his pretense—
more saucers, more cups in a far, dark
corner. He anticipates her descent, her head
below him, his subtle shadowed rush.

Her fingers curl. It does not matter if he
is grubby or sour or fat. There is no rock
at hand, no coiling snake, just cutlery
smooth and sharpened. How recently
she's left off her long johns, stopped wearing
her brothers' shoes. Her hand flies to
the knot at her waist, her tips forgotten;
in the square she begins the long walk home.

DADDY'S SONG

He has bought a new shirt, slipped it
from its cellophane sleeve, to please a woman.
The night birds stretch their necks and gargle
at the moon. Oh, love, love. He is not looking
at the stars, twisted like tinsel. They cost
nothing; they are too far away. He puts
a ring on her finger instead. The birds fly
to the family Bible, claw over its leaves.
New names are added to the march down the page.
The diagram deepens, widens—each child
a finger reaching, a leg, a piano key.
Light snow on the fields as he drives home;
dark lines of the earth winning through.
The night birds sing low and red.

THINGS I CAN KNOW
—Bill and Lou

The year my parents met, an earthquake rocked
Cleveland. Calvin Coolidge was President. Liquor
was smuggled from Canada in boats. The average
worker earned $26 a week. Lindbergh had yet
to cross the Atlantic, Trotsky had not yet
been exiled, and the Taisho Dynasty was about to end.
My mother was fourteen, just in from the country.
She shrugs off this encounter. Before they date,
Gandhi will be imprisoned, the stock market will crash,
and Edward VIII will abdicate his throne;
the planet Pluto will be discovered, Donald Duck
will appear in his first movie, and the Cleveland
Bloomer Girls will become national softball champs.

How much did a gardenia cost in 1938? My father
might remember. On Schaaf Road someone pinched
back the plants for weeks to coax my parents'
signature flower, glassed in under Cleveland's
cool skies. They drank Brandy Alexanders
and Pink Ladies; they danced like young trees.
Were breezy Fred and Ginger their models? Bonnie
and Clyde had already been shot dead. Before
they marry, child labor will be outlawed, cave
paintings will be discovered in Lascaux,
and the Seventh World's Poultry Congress
will convene in Cleveland. Germany will invade
Austria, Bohemia, Norway, war spilling over the world
like a kitchen accident hardening out of reach.

In 1945 Roosevelt dies, Hitler shoots himself,
the atomic bomb is dropped on Hiroshima. Bread
is 16 cents a loaf, coffee is 39 cents a pound,
and a man's suit costs $42.50. 11,945
marriages are recorded in Cuyahoga County.

My parents toast with champagne in the backyard
under a sycamore tree. In their photo—framed,
in the bedroom—my mother holds a cascade
of flowers, one for each night of their nuptial
drive to the South. My father still keeps
these honeymoon receipts in the family Bible.

Aunt Bella

It wasn't me who'd been married before, so I wore
white, scallops that echoed my hair. That's how
it was in the fifties, even though hanging around

the bar Thursdays and Fridays they told me
dirty jokes. I looked like a good-time girl—solid
with curves, a twitchy walk in heels, dyed hair.

What else was there to be, to do? I worked
with alphabetical cards in a box, a phone, dust
and paper in the files. My laugh filled up

the office and lingered in the corridor. I said
yes when he asked me—a man who felt the cold,
who needed love, who held his breath

against the endless night. I kept my job, but I kept
him, too. Like a short order house, I cooked eggs
over easy, burgers, used plenty of grease.

I made him warm, in bed and out, but it couldn't
last past my death. In the ground I turned over,
shrugged up my shoulder, laid my arm over my head,

pretending not to think about how he would be, less
and less of him until he entered the dark alone.

Eleven Years Later
—second cousins

Sundays are bad, the worst. Waking late, everyone
else in church clean and singing, and the Lord
answering back. Here in the too-warm sheets little

balls of fabric have been rubbing up all the years
since Janice has died. Howard cleans the house—
working toothpaste into the grout, oiling squeaks,

vacuuming the great desert reaches. All her stuff
is in the attic. It'll keep. No one's aching
to wear her pink quilted bathrobe or her too-tight

jeans. He can make a roast or meatloaf—cheery noise
of the grinder, orange scraps of carrot peel fly.
He turns away from the TV, the quack box.

All day the burlesqued shapes of men throw
themselves after the ball. You can get your teeth
into the news—something to talk about tomorrow,

even when the faces bleeding, crying, hidden
behind a raised jacket sleeve wouldn't seem
to belong around here. He and the smell of the meat

drift out to the garage. Down on the concrete floor,
it's cold. The car's been sluggish. It hesitates.
Leaking from an invisible nick, the engine

teaches him how he feels. The garage door whines
down against the careless flutter of leaves
blowing in from a bright day he wants no part of.

RECONSTRUCTION: LIST FOR THE A & P

Before supermarket as directive—the rhyming Stop
'n' Shop, the alliterative Pick 'n' Pay—when
automobiles (with voluptuous fenders) were fewer,
our mother's wired wheel carrier buzzed smoothly over
slate, hiccupped on bricks, humped down then up
each set of curbs on the way to the A&P. (Two blocks
away in the dark aisles of Fisher Food, home
of the impending vegetable, cans of peas and corn
lined up to roll down their chutes.) Oh, Great
Atlantic and Pacific Tea Company, men have shinnied
up trees to pick bananas, compared the lemon's rind
to the early morning sun, pulled pointing carrot
fingers clean from the soil; they have brought
the fruits of the world by truck, train, plane,
in primary colors, to this epicurean vortex, to be
funneled into these two brown bags, stacked
in the cart, pulled home and eventually spoon
(or fork) fed to the waiting mouths of the family.
Recombined, washed, basted or boiled:
                                        The largest
size bag of COFFEE beans—ground in the aisle (the good
earth from which each morning is sprung). Two dozen
EGGS if I'm to begin the Easter rolls. POPPYSEED.
WALNUTS. PRUNES. More KETCHUP. Look at the CHOPS.
BREADCRUMBS for meatloaf. CHICKEN ROLL for the girls.
OATMEAL. A head of LETTUCE. A can of MANDARIN
ORANGES (those succulent diminutives). What did *The Joy
of Cooking* say? 16 to 20 SMALL WHITE ONIONS. 1 pound
sliced MUSHROOMS. Stop in at Witthuhn's for new ivy plants
for bridge club. Leave note for an extra pint of cream.

RABBIT FOR SUPPER
—Meredith's story

I.

Closed, Egyptian-eyed beauty. She made love
a desert, his body hot and shifting—nothing
else lived. Driving to her house, muscling
the car up the last curve, watching her slide
onto the seat, her skirt cool and narrow,
her hair fluttering like reeds. His body
turns to that eye like a glyph speaking
its own language, marked with some darkness,
blue as a flood. He imagines pressing
his lips to the socket, beseeching.
Later there was the having, the bed
like a field of snow. Night hunting,
moon lover, her teeth leaving
an urgent tattoo on his arm.

II.

When he steps in from the cold clutch
of the day, from the sharp light and the trees
bleeding, the kitchen feels like a jar.
He holds the rabbit, dressed, already hung
towards tenderness. Spaghetti again. Backed
by the flat glow of the oilcloth and the open
mouth of a can, the steam gathers like wrath
around her unspoken scorn for the meat
and its bits of fur, its nearness to the earth,
the cold promise of blood drying on the skin.

III.

It's so early he can still see stars. Leaning
against his car, he waits for the foreman,
breathing in the hot, cloudy power

of the first cigarette, so good now,
before anything goes wrong. He thinks
about the job, a chance to use his body—
the clench, strain, pull—every day an anatomy
lesson about strength and resistance.

IV.

Johnnie's crowding him again, trying to make
him his brother. Hot whiskey and cold beer—
each man is fitted to his stool—split
knuckles and reinforced shoes. There's nothing
beautiful in the bar, only quarters
shining like small moons, and a nervous fizz
that rises like desire or fear. "That's
what a wife does," says Johnnie. "Scrapes
you down. Boils you in a pot. The kids
chew you for flavor."

V.

With his hand on her back as they dance,
that fretwork of muscle and bone
is a mystery all over again.
Their bodies press and retreat to music.

VI.

Their bodies thicken. Children fall out
and down. They become a bubble
of moderation. Their weapons and their eyes
dull. Their last dog dies. Johnnie
would say, "Is this life a piece of crap
or what?" But maybe love is laid down
like a layer of fat. Until the bones
poke through, they're surviving.

OH BITS: THE FLIP BOOK

It's a plane crash in the jungle. The drums
and birds go silent. The vocabulary
of death recedes like distant nickering bees.

complications   memorial   ash flake
devoted to her family   34 years at Ford

It must be dark just as it must be a journey.
The body is removed, the spirit already gone
to a sequin-sized glister on somebody's heart.

apparent heart failure   played the foot organ
dear sister   barber   truck salesman

Old photos are the labels off the can,
accomplished lives the seed packets
staked at the end of a line where
something new may be starting to grow.

sons and daughters   lifelong   cancer
born in Pikeville   born in Van Wert

In some Dante-esque pool they bob up, jostling.
They probe with an avid gardening shovel
and the enjoyable crochet hook. One last bulletin
of their virtues and the Bronze Star takes point.

He could stand on one hand on a stair rail.
She was clear and strong to the end.

A bent nun. A twenty-eight year old without
her stomach pain. They menace the dark with the open
pages of *A Child's Garden of Verses.*

died Thursday   worked in shipping and receiving
best known for his barbecued ribs

WITHOUT TONGUES: FAMILY STORIES

I. Safe as Houses

Under the sky, blue, gray, hazardous with rain,
her path erratic as a bee's, the dotted line
took her from house to barn to field, riding
Frank the ex-racehorse, the old sow one Sunday,
the brief high wave of her father's anger.
She gave it away. She put her hands up against
the low green smell, the milk, the dry cornfield
where another daughter had already been lost
in the blonde and russet shades. Thirty years
later, it's the fifties. She lives in a house
in a yard on a street. She paints its walls
and harrows its rugs. In this family there are
only two girls, one the sun shining, one more harsh
like the wind. They are put in the pantry,
egg-basted. They are baked together in a pie.

II. Replication

"How am I like Dad?" Do they really want to know—
whether it's painted on their genes or breathed in
from the cloud of body and ego heat we call home?
What could they discount? A nose is not a future.
Yes, maybe his nose before it was broken.
And the mouth; not his narrow, well-cut lips
but the things that are said without thought.
When I was twenty, I went to the wake of my aunt.
I was tall. I was young. I met an old woman
who stared up at me and said you look just like her.
I'd never been free, and the old woman put me
in a box, confined me to the squat horizon
of a low, dark room, the people murmuring.

III. Smoke Over the Land

When Cain and Abel were young—before the blood

and the marking—their father, whom the dogs
snapped at, would reminisce: about the animals
and their respectful gaze as he named them,
all that crap about the flaming sword, what God said
to him the last time. Eve, tired, ex-curvaceous
babe, couldn't chime in—how to explain
she wasn't paying attention when she took the fruit?
She'd felt dizzy, swayed. She was trying to think
what the snake reminded her of, if he'd be hot
and dry in her hand, when the juice, sweet
and familiar, woke her. In the new stories
the sun is harsh as well as warm, the clouds
are blown to rain, and the marks on our foreheads
say this is our home, let us stay.

MY SISTER'S RED PANTS, A FILM SHORT: 1953

Why am I wearing Mary's clothes? Already she is
the silent button, I am the crisp, metallic
snap. The rug is soft gray with the shape
of a leaf cut in. My hand rubs the nap, runs down
the hard waxed thread of the design. I rise up
by the chair, knees high stepping. I pull myself up
matching the too-long pants to the red chair.
The horizontal bar of movie lights swings up, too,
shifting darkness into corners the color
of February. Light means morning or mother,
but this brightness raised arm-high is shocking.
I knock the table into the wall on purpose:
the world is already awry. If the angel
of the Lord came and said, "Hail Mary,
full of grace," I could say not me. Not me
on a holy card. These pants are just one more prop
like the beach ball or the floppy hat or the edge
of the lake where I curl my feet away. Breaking up,
the isolated letters askew at the end of the film,
the white dots, the chain of white dots
like an ellipsis to the real world. That room
seems too empty, a flat place on a dark piece
of film with someone I don't know directing,
someone wanting another sweet incredulous laugh—
a boy who stole ice cream forty years before
while his mother entertained on the porch. I hope
it was peach ice cream with pieces of fruit
lined in red, glistening. Cindy Lou, soft
rubbed-off featureless doll, I am coming back
to pick you up. I am coming back to figure
this out. When I began. When I was not thoughtless
but unreserved. When love was not recognized
but given like a sweet scoop of apple on a spoon.

LITTLE PIES IN THE KITCHEN: 1959

It must be apple pie or tart because of my dress
like a picnic, red and white matching the fruit
(though its skin is missing)—the lemon-juiced fruit,
thin sliced, sugared, layered, with small gobs
of butter, cinnamon flecked. Aunt Minnie pops
her head in (not sitting down for coffee now),
just pops in her so-black puff of hair, rolls out
her smile and her slow stretching voice.
The kitchen juts out from the torqued spine
of the stair; the moon looks down at us
through double glass eyes. I know how to
stand, sit, be quiet—my mouth might almost be
wiped off! In the next room I have swelled, fevered,
spotted, hallucinated, been painted with calamine.
Now the scabs inside my elbows knit. Flour
is in the air. Twisting my nose to one side,
I roll out from the middle, slap the strips
and scraps back onto the pastry ball. The girl
with long brown hair washes the dishes, batting
away the tubular remains of a bobbing hot dog.
I sneeze, and the blast rushes like a storm
through the tunnels and canyons of mucous
membrane. It's a good thing we are not too wet
or greasy, not glutinous like the dough, dusted
with granules. Our flesh might toughen, absorbing
its own cloud of powders. Our bodies might
learn to separate from the threats and inducements
of the world. The kitchen is lit up like a stage—
yellow all around. The radio indicator points
to the door. Behind, the dark grilles of the oven
boom to the match. My eyes water. I cover my mouth.

IN SAECULA SAECULORUM: 1964

Crouched in a weird demented way by the spigot,
I am floating in a sea of instructions, parables,
steering away from all sin—avoidable rock-
splitting mortal, venial everywhere; I know
stories of virgins and martyrs, miraculous
rose in the garden, fingernails pulled in the woods,
one girl who preferred death. Prayer,
there should be a lot of this, and suffering
where we can't complain. Everything is in Latin
so it sounds better, the words filling
the mouth in exalted ways, the o's
like an orange promising juice, the tongue
humping up to the roof of the mouth as if
it were a cathedral. I am sitting in the dirt,
not scruffing joyously as the birds might. Inside,
my mother no doubt is making a sweet yellow cake,
hulling the strawberries, chilling the cream.
Maybe she's wrapping some little dreams for me
in the playroom. Maybe she's ironing my lavendar
swirl-skirted dress or listing how we need
more shampoo, more orange juice, more thick tan
supplemental Vitamin C, a liquid in control
of its globs and its globules. Maybe for three
minutes she sits down, she looks out the window
at nothing, she calls up my dad to bring home
a pack of Lucky Strikes. And me there in the dirt.
Not even proper dirt or big dirt, too neat
and flat and beaten, no mud or clods, just
the narrow strip between the house and the drive
behind the border of dead nettle where nothing
is growing. Marooned, I think of my self.
Others recede, boxed up like TV, far away
and faintly buzzing. Ordinary things—our porch,
the maple tree—pop up, loom like the plants
in time-lapse photography. Like some creature

from whom we accept one service—our life,
our freedom—the temptation of self hangs around.
I can't get rid of the scrounge, the lout,
the unctuous son of a snake and a swine. It oils
around, subhuman, like a hyena with its slanted
legs and horrible laugh, a riff on the bargain
we make. I say yes to my self for the first time.
I turn the wheel on the faucet, unloved, unloved,
each segment creaks past and releases the gush.

IN MEDIAS RES: 1965

Full-skirted, two-piece, all cotton pink
and white checked dress. Sleeveless. White
rickrack at the hem pointing. I wore it
in the schoolyard in May as a second violin,
having made my dog yowl for several years.
I scraped and plinked on a folding chair,
erect as if at the piano, with my hair,
serious, lifted in a bun. In the closet hung
a shiny pink sheath, a prelude to the real
thing, not yet tight, not yet strapless.
Faux slinky, something like Debbie Reynolds
might have worn under a mink before,
through the agency of a man, she learns
about real values. This is what the movies
said, also other immediate cues like pom poms,
black leather, the girl who takes off
her glasses and shakes down her hair. Besides
weekend movies on TV, I used to fasten
on the written word for clues: the "I Am
Joe's Organ" series in the *Reader's Digest*,
a photography magazine's out-of-context skin,
a *Saturday Evening Post* story I suspected
as particularly smutty involving an apron
and a woman of the woods. Flushed with youth,
arousal, shame, I suffered an affliction
of messages. At the drugstore lipsticks
echoed the flesh: natural, shell-berry-
rose-blush, the color of power diluted, mixed
intoxication of innocence and the ecstasy
of yet-to-be. And always a reminder
of their absence, clothes—button holes
that empty, skirts that narrow the focus,
elastic panels that deflect the thrust—
but that was a long way off. Clothes had
relaxed, fallen away, wrinkled, softened,
opened, before I better understood the parts
and how they fit together.

BOUND BY THE LAWS OF THIS WORLD: 1968

Blonde, blonde, blonde—there was a halo
melting around my head. Licking between
the chocolate wafers of an ice cream bar
in the lunchroom, I contemplated what Sister
had warned could be done with the tongue.
Listening, our faces had been smooth
as rain. But the smell of the earth
was thickening like incense. The swing
of the pleats brushed our thighs. We sensed
combustion, something breaking apart.
And the bars of the fire escape spelled
burn, reassembled, the iron steps leading
down from the deep lady blue of the sky.

     *   *   *   *

At fifteen, some girls are already women
in the way they dispose their limbs. They can
make their uniforms look slutty; they would never
be called to be mother to God. Their bodies
curve and fret like horses, heads tossing,
long slender legs, beautiful glowing rumps
like continents in vastness, in mystery.

     *   *   *   *

J.M.J.—I.N.R.I.—Not J.P. loves S.G.
Yes, Sister. I am a sister, too, a child
of God, a weak vessel, an unformed amphora
dried out in this sun, a tree rooted
in silence, sap curdling like phlegm
in my throat. Wand thin, I have
no magic. It's night. The celery-sick
walls rise up around me, the glass
in the door winks, as if it were still

the Middle Ages, and only this thought,
only this celebration may be lit up.

* * * *

Walking home from school, stopped
on the bridge above the river, legs angled,
arms braced on the rail, I'm an arrow looking up,
pointing at the eye of God, the clouds
brushed and gray like feathers. I'm not
interested anymore. The bridge, its triangles
hum behind me, under my feet. I'm waiting,
stretched, like that long piece of steel,
trembling, while everything else moves.

ADAM AND EVE AT THE PARTY

Having sent portents before me, I am called
through the air, anointed with blossoms. I am shiny
and straight as my hair. When I arrive, men bristle
and attend, disguising the secret outlines
of their olive drab. Thirsty for this experience,
I set aside taste, take the cup that is offered.
Does this make me wiser? Does this make me free?
My mouth won't stop smiling. Words take up more
space. Everything lifts with the axing
of hesitation, the unclipping of fear. My hair
floats down, sweeps over the nuts of the toilet,
the barely reclaimed white of the porcelain seat.
Oh, Bobby Jones, what words did you whisper, my eyes
rolling up, what sweet clean thing did you want
to save? Having tasted the apple, I lay under the sink,
the thick pipes curving above. Other guests needing
to piss were cast into the backyard darkness.

SURELY INCENSE AND MERCY WILL FOLLOW US ALL THE DAYS OF OUR LIVES

I.

Everything is contained in this one hour—the long
journey the woman makes, how her foot repeats
its step again and again; her filmy veil,
like gossamer, her veil like a film obscuring the slope
of her cheek and the craters without numbers on the already
dim path to the future. It's all in the walk down
the aisle: the altar that's really a table; behind,
the tree of redemption, the tree of the family of man.
It is her hardest work to put out her hand.

Black tux. White dress. Rice falls from the sky.
Four hundred ghosts whisper the vows, every lover
who believes for a moment until death do them part
takes these words. The families watch from opposite
sides. We might question their tears. Thrown
together they will bang, weighted balls on strings,
shock after shock de-escalating until they hang
quietly from their own predicaments.

II.

Rolled roast beef—projecting the early years.
Mashed potatoes, absorbing all juices
like a lumpy bed. *Halupke*—still meat
but ground, supplemented with rice, rolled
up in a gassy leaf. Green beans—will they ever be
more unknowing? The whole ceremony: corn. *Pizzelles*
like powdered sugar snowflakes, *kolachke*
with their fingernails of jam. The tiered
cake, as if we could wrap our sweetness in years.

III.

How white were my little girl socks, how ringletted

my hair. My hair, not wishing to call attention
to itself, faded back to flat. We four, intimate,
drank darkly suspect cherry pop at the weddings
of our 34 first cousins. What did it tell us
that mostly the women jiggled and stomped? Polka.
Csardas. They made a small happiness.

The men clustered in the bar or sat
with their legs spread, silently watching.
No one performed the apron death—exchange
of veil for kerchief, bouquet for broom.
The girl didn't roll into bed on cylinders
of quarters, she wasn't thrown by unfurling
dollar bills, the couple wasn't pronounced done,
popped out of a toaster like new bread.

IV.

At the dimestore downtown I choose a silverware
tray to carry back to our new half a house.
The crowd in the store hums and buzzes
like my blood. The cash register pings
with excitement. April day, and I'm riding
in a daze of fulfillment, sunshine gushing
like love through the bus window, the engine breathless.

I pant in the sheets, the artfully twisted
sheets, my bedroom eyes, my just-woken-up
seductive bedroom eyes. The sheets, blue and white
checked, are not right for this scene. Christ,
this expected scene! I'm here like the furniture
which is all second hand, the couch that coughs
foam dust, the metal-legged kitchen table
and chairs like monkeybars. I'm crying
like a girl, but nobody's watching.

V.

Is there something sinister about the bridal
party, how they dress like interchangeable parts?
She holds onto the litany of promises,
the priest's instructions as he looks over
her head. She's equipped—her womb ticking
like a bomb, the handholds of her breasts,
twin magnets above the ultimate resting place.
The man always returns to the woman. Is this
her triumph? Their skins blossom with love.

THE PEELING AWAY OF HANDS

Swallowing her usual advice, Mother surprises
me in her birthday call telling the great
gawky oldness of me how she remembers

me small, home from school, slipping into her lap
just to sit. I imagine the dangle of skinny legs—
myself an event in my mother's life:

how she brought me home with a too-big head,
how for forty-three years she's handled
the hovering, the peeling away of hands.

Growing up, direction is easy, our bodies
an instructive ladder—arms and legs
point up, the curved foothold of the pelvis,

the crosspiece of each rib. Out of the prison
of custom and age we vault from the heart.
Thirteen years ago, a green Horizon hurtled

through the rain, the outside May morning
a blur of whispering, licking water.
In the delivery room, my body,

acting on its own, against itself,
held the child in with an extra loop
of the cord. Now that child pulls away,

progressively avoids the lap, the arm,
the hand. At night on the couch while
we watch TV, he places a pillow against

my protruding body parts before he leans.
My face in repose is fairly wrinkle-free,
but webs are the new instruction.

The body no longer imitates a ladder
but a web like a hand to hold on. Here
at the center when I kiss him good night,

I make smacking bird noises or dig
a little with my chin to disguise
the silk-strength, the abundance of my love.

OEDIPUS AT CLEVELAND:
BECOMING UNKNOWN

Fuck Oedipus and all he's done to screw up
family love. Mom's no Jocasta, queening around,
sharpening her brooch. Dad still journeys
forth in his chariot, quarreling at crossroads.
There's no city at issue, chorus of witnesses,
curse; no oracle of birds and bones, no blind
man biting his tongue. Still the boy defeats
his parents, deepens his voice, grows snarly
as underarm hair. Darkling, he edges around
their life, starving, incredulous. He accepts
food offered at arm's length. Breast meat
pulled from the bone. Milk. Scrambled
eggs already salted, peppered. Cucumber
disks, green rimmed, on a clear glass plate.

STATIC ELECTRICITY

Black ribbed cotton pants a little baggy
at the knees, the purple high tops that I
love—I stand outside the dressing rooms
like the sad end of winter. I can only try
on hats. This one cuts becomingly across
my forehead. I imagine a need for it,
a climate, my coat and twenty pounds shed.
I take it off and on, I look in each mirror
waiting for my daughter and her jeans,
hearing the clerk and a young woman discuss
static cling: the sleeveless, champagne-colored
top molds across her stomach in an unkempt
way. I try on my hat. Should I turn,
stodgy in my brown coat? I could say
*handcream, stroked underneath on your middle
and thighs.* I stand with my flesh melting
around me, everyday more skin, less hair.
I am as dry as the air. How old am I
that I should give advice, interrupt
with my important news. I take off my hat
and call to Kate, frantic for a life
too crowded for chat in a store, telling
more than all want to hear. I come clean,
tell how the cream drapery could hang unbent.
Random noise. Obstruction. Old piece
of rayon wrinkled and spent, rubbed
across the carpet of the world, me
all negative, the earth positive in mission
and charge. My hair stands on end.

SELF-PORTRAIT: NOTES

The tiny square of a yellow kitchen glows
like a lunch box on the far shore of the lake
at its darkest green; ghostly plantings of corn

there, smokestacks and a sooty flue with resplendent
blue flame; a woman with long brown hair, with wings,
flies in the trees. Baptism into this landscape

by total immersion was so long ago I'm not even wet
as I race forward—fearing to be turned into
three flowers and an orange—menaced by the tower

of books beginning to curve toward me, one hand
held back to fend them up. My ugly foot is not
forward; it's hooked by quotation marks pounded

into the present field like croquet hoops; bits
of words, syllables empty out of my ear. Sketch in
the beautiful color of the hair—the faint

dark line at its part, the shaped eyebrows, the good
nose with a dent of concentration above, always
an earring dangling. But I think to make this picture

I would have to lose ten pounds—how much weight
does the poem add? I have to be wearing black—
no rich brocade spooning the curve of my hips—

a mirror with my real face in the hand careless
at my side obscured by a dusty upgrowth of false
sumac fronds. Something I'm buttoning up

(or down) on top—the tattoo of a man's hand just
shows, his finger touching my heart. But now I have
three arms like an Indian statue; already

grotesque, add another stretching back like Alice at her most resilient to a boy and girl turning away to a different horizon. They're waving.

Perpetual Motion/Day of Rest

Orchestrate the shuffle of feet, the Fahrenheit
dial, the drift of steam. *We are here.* "Bring

a card table and three more chairs." A joyful
concentrate of kitchen sweat shines

on our faces, a blast of bourbon syrups
our sounds. "Drain the carrots and beans"—

pot lids tilt over the sink—"who's watching
the rolls?" The first bite of mashed potato,

the last drop of gravy in the boat! *We're
alive. We're eating.* No lone drumstick

remains. Dessert calls from the kitchen—*Good
Housekeeping* recipes made flesh—lime fluff

with its tufts of angel food, the grainy
gestures of poppyseed cake. "Don't pour till

the coffee's settled." The shouts, the retold
stories—Aunt Sylvie's finger pokes my arm.

We are here. We are here. "This blouse
cost only a quarter." "Do you remember when I threw

the pies?" "And then she said, he's not the man
I married." Every seventh day it repeats;

the whipped cream trembles like a mountain,
the cookbook is peaked like a shrine.

III

NATURAL ACTS

It's spring. Forgotten white tulips gleam
like eggs under the evergreen. Narcissus
fan out their leaves. Hyacinths straggle
and tilt, stumpy with florets, heavy with scent.

The man who jumped from his own window—
cars look as they pass by, wonder who
is that man, although they never wondered
before. He's face down on the grass.
Only his shoes show under the white cloth.
The policemen all point up, discuss the natural
act of a man flying, dropping like a bird
from the nineteenth floor. Now the earth
will cover him. Each spring will tug
at his body more, molecule calling to molecule.

Maybe cable TV is a good thing. It dulls
the self, pretends about the world—
that it's not new, that virgins are not
surprised by pain. The newspaper reports
on three teens, triangle in the front seat
of a stolen car. When the policeman
flashed his blue lights, chased the car
to an impasse, two of them died for love,
the girl left spattered with blood,
cheated of her death pact share. Someone
should have told them life is bearable.

EVERY BAD THING THAT COULD HAPPEN

On a plane, the absurdities of our undertakings
can be more apparent. Look where we are—
rising above the clouds like the steam on soup.

The round cloud tumuli make an insubstantial
floor, floating like the opaque reaches
of the brain. Copper flash of river. Broken

mountain spine. The road below trunks and branches
like a lizard, a creature drawn to appease
the whirring visitors of the night. Everything

feels small: the square of bread in cellophane,
the toilet's bottled soap and slots for waste,
the cabin's used-over air. I don't want

to imagine angels outside, a choir of them,
a nation, dipping their heads as we fly by
drinking Cokes and tomato juice. I don't want

to imagine our journey as an overheated flight
in the belly of a bird tensed to make a last bloody
descent. The locating light on the tip

of the wing dips and bends in the dark. Liquids
roll in my head. Down there, sidewalks have mica chips
like stars. Down there, rushing over the surface

like shadows with wings we are still believing,
flying. Down there, we close our ears to the noise;
the essential shrieks of reason and fear become a drone.

THINNING DOWN

They sleep with their mouths open—a curious cave
with drip tide and sonorous roar. The skin
thins down to air mail, wrinkles becoming
almost irrelevant as long as the loose
slip holds. The kidneys give, the bladder
hesitates. They're increasingly interested
in the soap opera of the bowel, its sulky
withholding, the moans, the intemperate
rush to release. All but the seventh veil
have dropped: beauty, bloom, hair, appetite,
reason, wit. If only this process was a journey:
one could light out, stow away, jump ship.
But "overboard, overboard!" They can't breathe,
their arms and legs are as weighted as prayer.

NINETY-FIRST BIRTHDAY WISH

I want to believe in reincarnation: next
year or the spring after, my parents
could come back as young twin deer. Not

fauns which sounds too mythical—they'd
want to be furred, physical and wild,
able to browse through ivy beds and drink

from bird baths throughout this outlying
half-overbuilt suburb of green cake
squares and flowering pie wedges

end-crusted with trees, where each blade
of grass is an assurance that this is home
even if you can't see them living.

For the hoof-click, they could exchange
the rubber-cane-tip-pock. Already they have
the same awkward tilted persnickety walk

canted forward as if to listen for danger.
They need to be stretched and quickened. They
need the deep chest and the muscled haunch.

LIMBO: THE DUTIFUL RETURN

I. Disclaimer

Long day, long day. Her body drowns, draws
in on itself so the world may be forgotten.
Tired, lying down, drawing her legs up
at last from the floor.
                      I am here again,
the first home, between the index finger
and the opposable thumb. Everything I am
is a result of that grip. The mother
and father lie down, they make a child,
they keep it in a crib with bars, a cradle
designed to keep it off balance. No matter
what is taught, it's the wrong thing. Returning
I have climbed back into the toybox knowing
the danger of shutting the lid. The bed,
the stove, the loaf of bread like a little house.

II. Long, Broad, and Sharpsight: a Fairytale

In the world of two sexes, we must assemble
our skills—our beauty, simplicity, wits.
We can travel the length, devour the breadth.
We can spy the smallest jewel or acorn.
And then the measure of the eye begins
to fail; the clear eye, the long sight,
one seeing near, one far; the iris like a shield
on a small white globe, a continent
whose mysteries are about to lessen. Outside
a bird calls, passionless, uninflected.
Night becomes one of the tasks we must
master: keep breathing, wake up, laugh.

III. Refrain

I am not a hunter, but I have seen

someone tremble, look away,
surrender the privacy of the self
to the ministrations of the world.
Afterward, when I call his name, will he
still answer?

              Long day, long day. Her body
drowns, draws in on itself so the world
may be forgotten. Tired, lying down,
drawing her legs up at last from the floor.

SECRETS OF MURANO

Sand—this is a hint how the world works.
The long breath of the glassblower shapes

the gob, still fluid, warm, a long
stream of event and feeling. I imagine

a thermometer, the red going up, a spoke-
like tube. Time hiccups, breaks. Bits

of the past fall like Venetian beads.
That breath rushing forward like a song,

the sweep of it—I don't need this to be
God's wind, a furnace divine. But how much

it feels, at the end, as if some hand breaks
off the bulb, picks up the miniature

scene and shakes, the snow heaving
and falling unnaturally quick and breathless.

RECRUITS AT FORT STARK

The TV is a square of relentless desert light,
the land lying down open to the sky, each
butte an altar; as portents of rush, gust,

puff, and change, the effortful dust and message-
laden smoke. The strong dark line, the double
file turn of the mounted column rides;

each horse like a nerve jumping—arch, gloss,
speed and sheen—all that horses stand for.
My father is walking with John Wayne when

they were young—that swagger in Cavalry pants.
At the edge of the country, at the edge
of the river, the white tents rise, hopeful

as pyramids. "This coffee is weak, but
it's all we have." "Singer, sing out to forget
your thirst." "Bugler, sound the charge." My father

and I watch, and the story pours into our sore
empty places. Children are rescued. The arrow
in Wayne's chest is pulled out by his son. My hand

is ready, but there's no shaft to the matter sticking
into my father's heart. John Wayne steps onto the dirt,
dashes the dregs of his coffee onto the ground.

EVENING MEDICATION

white pill melting on my tongue   no no
dissolving   misshapen tooth with no bite
left   I take it out   push it into the sky
where it shines   in the head's dark
hemisphere   walking down the road   so happy
    I dance a little in the starlight   in the moon
shine   my knees bend   my ankles thrust
    my breath puffs regular in its little
cloud   thoughts snapping   lighting up
like a room   swaying away like headlights
on a curvy road   oh breath   oh skin
    me flaking apart in a dusty trail
like the Milky Way   clouds gauzy in the night
sky   in my dark clothes   everyone else
at home   muscles pull up the small rise   I am
not afraid of the leaves barrow-shaped
at the curb   of the black mask of the rustling
shape in the ditch   am I   eyes clear
    the pupil spreading for the night   lifting
my face up to this moment   I know
there's nothing to kiss   lips   breath
    breath   the lungs like snowflakes
    the pill's bitter milk   the cold white sheets

THE DREAM OF SOUP

I didn't know it was her last meal.
Maybe I hustled her along. I was standing;
I hate doing the spoon thing. I was impatient
with her dying. I—I—I—. I expected
it would take some many more months.

The ancient idea of soup to sup or sip—
a soupcon. Old crone with a pot. Keep it
hot at first, parsley fogging with particles
the true promise of two. *Mary and Sue*
please. Take this cup from me.

We didn't know how. All summer and fall and winter
she sat pointed at the stove waiting with her new soup
spoons, the last objects that pleased her, anticipating
the melting cheese, the ocean of broth, her cup
emptying into herself again and again.

When I returned, pulling back the curtain at the door
that hid her dying, the air had already become
unpalatable. She'd come back so many times,
did I mind she couldn't wait? Leg flung up
casual, heart still pumping blood.

Months before, her ghost terrorized me: I think
I'm awake lying on my side, my knees drawn up.
Mother glides in, drapes over me. She weighs
nothing, gauze. She's the color of clothesline,
her shade so cold I'm afraid to check her bed.

Even the fun of that is gone now. At the end,
she says, "tell me about the kids"—quick
fair streams where her blood still flows.
"Give me more of the soup. Keep the rest
warm on the stove for your father."

The afternoon is a dark piece of cheese intent on transforming. *I lie down under the crematorium sky and ask for flame. Reduce me to ash, release me to fly lighter than air. I am too tired to sleep.*

BLUE

There was a different kind of drowning
in the emergency room, a different kind of wave,
the curtain blue and billowing, its netted

top, the hooks by the ceiling. Cranked
by a handle, suspended on sheets, your body
doesn't think much of itself. For a minute

it's eager to leave. The ears disconnect,
the eyes cloud; paper and tubes help you
live. The wheelchair is your car—but no

tumultuous incline, just inch, inch, inch.
*The song of old age is singing, the bell
in the ears has been ringing alarm.*

Something dissolves as I float, my throat
twisting. I try to project from my body
to yours: pool-sun-sky, blue under blue,

the body loved by water, each skin cell
cool, the eyes wrinkling, lungs eager
to breathe; muscles flutter, reach,

snap like the best fish in the world.
*Waiting for you, waiting for you to decide,
there's a long wait. I wait for you.*

Making the world smaller, you try
to crawl up the spiral to home—how it was,
how it was. Oh the past, the golden haze

of your youth in decay. Sepia—it sounds like
disease; the brown tint lurks in the sky
like pollution, rushes down when the moment

is over to wash it in fixative. Road dust,
the car's in reverse, the lost satisfactory
round of the wheel with its finger grips.

And if the present is night, the mind's eye
blue with distance? If that taste is a long
drink of water gathering shadows in the cup?

Sunday, Late April Snow

Cold color of unearthed potatoes,
a vichyssoise of vapor that I drive
through this last time. The engine
climbs through its registers
of power, climbs the ticking, clogged
steep of the present to the emptiness
of my parents' last home. In the yard
a magnolia collects shiver-brief
lickings of snow, pink exhalations
over petals breathless as the jot
of the past where the child
who was my mother runs barefoot
to the springhouse, each step prickling
a cold clear kiss that says she's alive.

My Parents Comment on Art

I.

Because mess and message have the same root
no story coiled, opened, flowered in the seamless
installation of plenty that was my parents' home.

Boy had already met girl. Any dust sprinkling
down from the rubbed-over plot line could be
hoovered away. There was the daily egg sketch,

the rabbit-eared TV's vaulting line. We
were taught the purifying lap and layer, like Christo,
of public toilet seats. Because they believed

in representational living, it was very late
when my mother studied the vanishing point
and embraced Van Gogh's bloated, crooked line.

II.

The couch picture: the old world hung
on the wall for fifty years: serene edgeless
clouds like armchairs, groups of leaves,

even the building stones are rounded. Turned
to each other in friendship, two featureless
women pause on the first approach to the bridge.

III.

In the hospital—second round—serene
is downgraded to bland. Next to the plastic
bracelet, Dad wears his watch, screwing

his eye around its cloud of cataract to check
on the flight of time. He hallucinates

the TV on fire, a man with burns being taken away.
Horrible, Dad says, with a flushed hectic
relish. I try to put out the fire. Was that wrong?
We're all burning with oxygen. Maybe we're lit

like the tips of forbidden cigarettes. I talk
about the lawn mower, sprinkle the imagined
green on the luscious and powerful red.

    IV.

Something has been omitted . . . Look . . .
The full circle of the story has been squashed,
the home in the shape of an egg. For his cloistered,

radiant faces, Vermeer boxed the world in the window,
kept it at bay by the door. It became a point
of order like that. The car always ran,

the furnace heated, the kitchen burgeoned to feed
the family of four, the small round dots
of their mouths full, the small round dots

of their eyes. The whole point was there
should be no story but the past—snake
handling on the highways, Uncle George jumping

out of his shoes. Point-blank: our parents
are dead. They have achieved the point of no return.
Their objects fan out like their commingled dust.

IV

INSIDE OUT

There is something so clean about the outdoors.
Consider that I have to name this in reference
to a structure, always in reference
to a wall—its in-side, its out-side, its door,

open or shut. The wind is behind the trees,
lying back on the lawn catching
his breath from blowing the moon out. But
if we are already outside where would the light

go? Around, I suppose. And if the moon is out,
it is lit, but if blown out, it's not.
What I like about the outside is its neatness.
If a bunch of stuff, leaves for instance, falls

on the ground, but even a dead bird or the wing
of a butterfly or an animal carcass,
it can be blown away or covered or steamed
and puddinged and transformed. Seeds fly

through the air, drop from the bodies of birds
and nobody has to clean them up. They grow
or fester into something else. This
is what's so different on the inside of the wall.

Everything remains the same. It has to shine,
it has to serve. But what about redecorating?
What about rusted bedsprings or broken
TV cabinets on the tree lawn on trash day?

They sagged or lost a leg and wouldn't be new.
They wouldn't remain. Often we think
about spring being new. Snowdrops, the first
shoots and buds, that green ground haze,

the purpling red of the trees that can be seen

from a distance. It feels new after winter
when even the light was at a different angle,
the way everything was broken down

so it could be again. You know, earlier,
the wind resting on the grass? We want to think
that about the wind because we're lonely.
If the sun were a chariot rolling up the sky,

we'd be sharing rules. The same language,
the same expectations would apply
on both sides of the wall. Think of the page
as a little house, each stanza a room.

We are conservatives about heat, energy,
youth, the kind of particles that float
in our air. Even knowing better, don't we
think of the sky as a great vaulted roof?

Ranunculacious

after a print by Michael Loderstedt

As soon as a dog shows up in a poem, powdery
brown, hairy as a coconut, my eyes
start to roll back into my head. Leashed
sensualists who engage the world, dogs
are better than cats who arch and yawn
in commentary, undulating like a bowl
of superior cream. Side by side like the lion
and the lamb, like the earth and ether—tawny
loam and smoky phantasmagoric white,
they are bad missionaries from the world,
we panting here still dogged and selfish.
Strike all but their colors, flat-rendered
like the globe smashed on the page, art
gone vegetable—spore, pit, pip, grain,
nut; germ on the ground and its ghost
in the air. One is the I, two the seed;
join the five senses and the twelve apostles
of thought, acrobatic in their mysteries
and apprehensions. Cork, boat, ball and cup, bull's
eye, bulb discovered in the grids of attention.

HARSH SUMMER DAYS

Lo, now, the summer's heat comes down like pollen,
golden and choking, waves fuzzing eyebrows,
ball caps, settling into the crease of their mitts.
Behind the chain link fence, the children are numbered,
distanced. Their hearts thud beneath the block
capitals of "French's Funeral Home," "Harold's
Oil 'n' Lube." The fence, that vast cellular wall,
is permeable to the taunts and exhortations
of the crowd. But even when we don't see it,
it's still there. The fence ripples like a wire
school of fish. Each compartment holds
a day, an hour, an Ur-game, the appearance
of movement locked into place. Caught in each
segment, embedded, a child ripens. The fence
and its wicked shimmering—it throws off
a wordless shout of light. We spectators
hood ourselves, put our hands up against it,
squint to find some relieving darkness inside.

PARTICLE-DROP-BREATH-RAY

Sea weed, flexible walleye bones, empty
shells, draggled gull feathers. Rain falls
like the color of the sun, accumulates.

Two-legged, stripped down to essentials (but
not too far), we wade into the water, reverse
ice to the drink, the waves trying to wear us

down, longing to serve us up like pips
on this margin of melted beach. The wind whistles
through our teeth, the sand grinds them down.

In the honeypot of the sun, headache-y, blasted
with thirst, we should be learning about excess,
the salt coming up to crust us as if each beach

were the ocean. We genuflect with our beads
of sweat to the salt whisper and the shelving
tongue that made us, here at the crux—the sun

like a peach above our glowing convoluted heads,
bodies of water swaying, our feet momentarily
stilled in the scratchy reactive electric fuzz.

THE WILDCAT LASHES ITS TAIL

We did not live on its shore. We did not navigate
its streams. When we learned to swim in my century,
we rode two buses to the Y and bubbled

and churned in chlorine. But the lake—blue
scallop darker than the sky, cold smile
from the astral plane, sly tongue curvetting

between two buildings—waits. White caps snap
on the surface, white skulls roll underneath.
The foolish slip into the lake with the wise—

wearing two sets of clothes, crossing the ice
on boards. The islands are named as comforts
and warnings—Rattlesnake, Little Sister, Starve

Island. Lie on a bed of ice, eyes closed, never
moving until you can't feel the cold. Imagine
as the waters close over your head. The black

of your skirt billows up like a thundercloud.
Between the sun and its glint, the cursive
mumble of the waves suggests all the parts

of a snake, black lines that slither like tongues
edging towards their teeth. Long before LaSalle
sailed west, his ship risen from the forest,

disappearing into the waves, a figure was carved
into rock—sea lynx, underwater manitou.
In 1931, packed into a hoax of a box on the shore,

Erie's serpent was captured—"seen in smooth waters,"
"it appeared to be playing." People said it was twenty feet
long, men clubbed it and dragged it to shore. Now,

no one will lift the lid. Erie, old gouge, slipper-shaped
before there were shoes, false remedy to the lesson
I cannot learn—that all is dust—new parable, too.

ELEGY FOR MYSELF AS A SURFER

At forty-one, my body a faulty missile aimed
at the shore smashed into the pebbly grind, half-
peeled of its suit. Avast, adrift, abrupt,

annihilated. In a kind of swoon, my mind disposed
of by the jumble of sensation, the cessation
of balance. That the body should feel such delight!

Me, a living flotsam doing rings around
my own inner ear. Oh, the undulations of the swells,
swells, swells.
            When I was all cartilage, pliant
as a shark, girls with two-piece suits in movies
posed on their boards and plucked bouncy plaintive
music on the beach. I drifted on a blow-up raft,

maybe with an idea of paddling to Canada, passive-
aware of the coconut oil illusion not total
immersion, that briny Pacific gasp.
                                    I want
to believe like Piaf when she sings of regret,
making her rough way up the steps of her charged
dismissals; I want to say, "Me, too." But now

the smallest part of me, the one sandy grit
left in the whorl of my ear, knows if Ohio
hadn't combed my hair so smooth, I could have been
a surfer girl.
            I wade into the water, only my head
above the platter of Lake Erie, not a landscape where
Venus would arise against the flushed luminescent

shell of evening here, next to the trailer park.
A bird presses against its billow of air;
the jets splash their icy beads even higher.

Behind me my flip-flops on the hard beach
and the waves hissing in a satisfying way, curling
like a frenzied bed of watercress doing salaams.

Even Farther Downstream from Shalott

My hair is too short to braid, no draperies for the hard
bench where I'd have to recline singing, the annoyance
of the employees in their neat blue shorts the cost

of this gesture. The ferry goes forth. Windless,
the rain begins. Moving toward smoothness, oblivion—
mist, moat—carried on the water, enclosed by the twisted

ropes of its fall, I become invisible as the fish
flecking the swells like caraway. No mirror here, no brazen
greaves; the unseen clouds plume up in the bodiless

sky. I have been saved by no agent. I am not about to be
born. Peril like a hook may slide toward me, its metallic
taste filling my mouth, but still on this death barge,

this pleasure boat, I blush the inexplicable pink tinge of joy.

ROADSTAND (TWENTIETH CENTURY FRUIT)

Peach tree orchard—a loose kind of pleasure.
In the spring, a peignoir of blossoms slips off.

A few warm nights. The air hums. Somewhere
two mouths tremble together. Then, as if knees

hit the ground, there's the groaning
with fruit, juice everywhere, the branches

bowed, held up with clothes poles.
They're such short trees for all that drama.

FROM THE SANDY BOTTOM OF LAKE ERIE: THE G. P. GRIFFITH

In fairy tales, sometimes the favored mite travels
in a walnut shell with a pinch of cotton fluff,
some string, a geranium leaf shade. Or imagining,

we might launch a loose curl of bark, placing inside
the figure whose eyes and mouth we've embroidered,
the nostrils so small we cannot stitch open

their pepper flakes. But the dead, life-size,
did not embark on a saucer, forget-me-nots
for an anchor and chain. Greased pieces of metal,

lissome teak barques carried coal, flaxseed, flour,
barrels of whiskey or apples, package freight. Ships
heavy with quarry, women laden with gold. Some

held their breath when they stepped aboard. Some
dreaded the tilting flat on the way past Fairport,
Erie, Silver Creek. Ships can founder, explode,

break up in the heavy chop. Under the white caps,
walnut timbers roll. Boys drift home naked, encased
in ice. Pretending to be as generous as air,

the lake laps feet, watercolors a sunset path
to faith. It is 1850. They step aboard, futures
sewn into their immigrant seams. When night falls,

when the breeze lifts the hair off their warm
June necks, the sparks from the cargo hold fly.
Steering for shore, run aground a half mile out,

the ship begins its burn to the waterline. Hundreds die,
gulping their prayers or choking the sidewheels.

Lockets round their necks, seed in the hold,
are they fish that they should swim, islands
that they might float? In the morning, bonnets,
pocket knives—attendant kickshaws strew the beach.

Should they have stepped away, not struggled
with hull wood or boiler stoke? But the body
itself is a curious packet with a raucous

lamentable crew. Even before our first alien breath,
in the initial watery home, it was all voyage, surprise.

GHOSTS

How many times did I waken confused, the sound
of the wind in the leaves, a summer sound, restless,
the green at its most extravagant, chlorophylled,

the droops and plumps and tapering that can hide
a bird. Before they got up, before I counted
the ceiling tiles, I would think it the sound

of the waves—no human voice can call so well—
at Catawba, returning so many times
we wore the linoleum away. Hamburgers, frozen

custards, the enticing TV dinner with segmented
tray. Sweet corn stripped of its leaves, the golden
teeth grinning. Cheesecake from the island store,

rich on its salver of foil. Nobody fished. We never
went in a boat. We swam, plunging and drenching
two times each day. Once, at dusk, our hair

already dimming in the air, the pink of our sunburn
sliding away, we entered the lake in our clothes.
I remember that puckery cotton, lavendar

and white, darkening, from the bottom up,
in the whispering clamor. There are currents
everywhere, some marked, some faithful. Feeling

their pull even now, I see how Mother stretched
their love an extra generation that I might reach
this century with still some muscle and egg.

LAKE ERIE LOVE SONG

From the road, the identical fishing shacks
look so small one mystifies how to fit a bed inside—
pulled down from the wall at night? She sings
with the windows open, a box of fudge on the table,
the sweet grit of it still in her teeth. He hoses
down table and pails, the uncertain skitter of fluids
and scales dribbling away. Together, the highball
glasses clink. She leaves her lipstick mark
while bourbon blows a last gust of the day's heat
down their limbs. Outside, the slap of the waves,
the water's gems and metals snarled with light. Inside,
the rub of the sheets, the body ever willing
to repeat its story. Some peaches and the coffee cups
with a green stripe wait on the sink until morning.

MAINSTREAMING THE BODY'S METAPHOR

Dismissing the earth with its steady grip, our feet
push off to do their dance in air. And that air,
faithful, rushes into our lungs, tickles our nose

hairs. Because air is invisible we believe in it
like God or justice, its hidden unplumbed
depths no part of this planet. When water

disappears, it must pelt tempestuously back
to earth. Stick your head in and it seems clear
it's not our medium; rubbery depressed

bubble-words bump but no longer fit the ear. Like
the sailor who drinks his own death glass
after glass, we seek the illusion of control,

our fascination a kind of eating with the eyes,
like calling to like, our tears becoming their own
pools, our mouths watering with hunger or greed.

Just so the lake is forever swallowing its own. We fix
a boat on the splash, a floating world where dry
can triumph, but dry can only follow drain.

Imagine our boat moored, dropping down, dangling
sideways like a rubber stopper if the lake's
unplugged down to its rug of dirt. Landlocked

metaphor leads to confusion. See the water insistent
in its jitter and spread, the lake's angstical
gyrations opposing the unfelt push of the air?

Forget the mystery of bulge, tip, and rump. Think
interior like a geode. Break open the body
to study firefly fish sparking the currents of blood.

About the Author

Susan Grimm lives in Cleveland, Ohio. *Lake Erie Blue* is her first full-length poetry collection. She is also the author of the chapbook *Almost Home* (Cleveland State University Poetry Center). Her writing has appeared in such publications as the *Plain Dealer, Rattapallax*, and *Spoon River Poetry Review*. She is a recipient of an Ohio Arts Council fellowship in poetry and the Ohio Poet of the Year Award from the Ohio Poetry Day Association. She teaches at Cleveland State University.